NATIONAL LEAGUE EAST

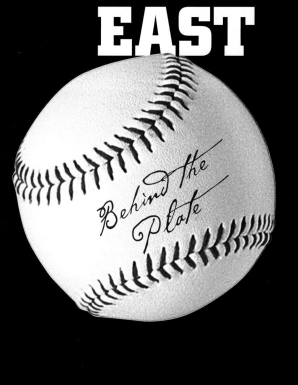

Behind the Plate

By Michael Teitelbaum

THE ATLANTA BRAVES, THE FLORIDA MARLINS, THE NEW YORK METS, THE PHILADELPHIA PHILLIES, AND THE WASHINGTON NATIONALS

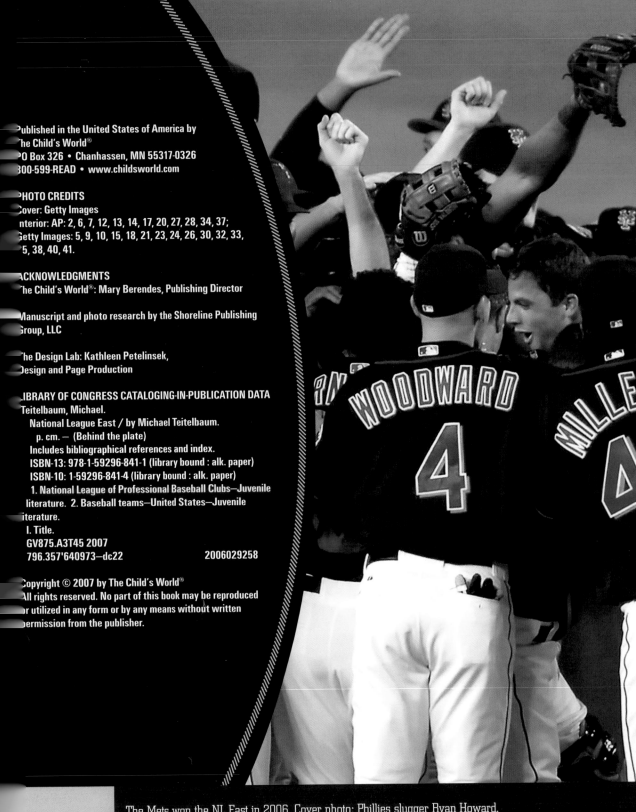

Published in the United States of America by
The Child's World®
PO Box 326 • Chanhassen, MN 55317-0326
800-599-READ • www.childsworld.com

PHOTO CREDITS
Cover: Getty Images
Interior: AP: 2, 6, 7, 12, 13, 14, 17, 20, 27, 28, 34, 37;
Getty Images: 5, 9, 10, 15, 18, 21, 23, 24, 26, 30, 32, 33,
35, 38, 40, 41.

ACKNOWLEDGMENTS
The Child's World®: Mary Berendes, Publishing Director

Manuscript and photo research by the Shoreline Publishing
Group, LLC

The Design Lab: Kathleen Petelinsek,
Design and Page Production

LIBRARY OF CONGRESS CATALOGING-IN-PUBLICATION DATA
Teitelbaum, Michael.
   National League East / by Michael Teitelbaum.
      p. cm. — (Behind the plate)
   Includes bibliographical references and index.
   ISBN-13: 978-1-59296-841-1 (library bound : alk. paper)
   ISBN-10: 1-59296-841-4 (library bound : alk. paper)
    1. National League of Professional Baseball Clubs—Juvenile
   literature. 2. Baseball teams—United States—Juvenile
   literature.
    I. Title.
   GV875.A3T45 2007
   796.357'640973—dc22   2006029258

The Mets won the NL East in 2006. Cover photo: Phillies slugger Ryan Howard.

Contents

4   INTRODUCTION

7   CHAPTER ONE
     THE ATLANTA BRAVES

14   CHAPTER TWO
     THE FLORIDA MARLINS

21   CHAPTER THREE
     THE NEW YORK METS

28   CHAPTER FOUR
     THE PHILADELPHIA PHILLIES

35   CHAPTER FIVE
     THE WASHINGTON NATIONALS

42   STAT STUFF

45   GLOSSARY

46   TIMELINE

47   FOR MORE INFORMATION

48   INDEX

48   ABOUT THE AUTHOR

INTRODUCTION

Fourteen years is a long time by almost any definition, but it is practically an eternity in today's baseball world. With so much coming and going of players and coaches and executives in the modern era of free agency, it's almost unheard of that one franchise could be so dominant for so long. But the Atlanta Braves were, winning 14 consecutive division titles from 1991 to 2005 (there were no official division winners in the strike-shortened 1994 season). That included every National League (NL) East crown since the division took its current five-team form beginning in 1994.

Finally, in 2006, the New York Mets broke Atlanta's stranglehold on the division. The Mets deftly mixed a blend of talented youngsters and playoff-tested veterans to win the East with ease.

There's a lot more to the history of the NL East than just the Braves' dominance and the Mets' **resurgence**, however. The Braves, in fact, weren't even a member of the East when the division originally was formed in 1969 (somehow, they were lumped in with teams in the West). That was the year the NL grew from 10 teams to 12 and split up into two divisions for the first time.

NATIONAL LEAGUE EAST TEAMS:

Atlanta Braves
Founded: 1871
Park: Turner Field
Park Opened: 1997
Colors: Navy blue and garnet red

Florida Marlins
Founded: 1993
Park: Dolphin Stadium
Park Opened: 1987
Colors: Aqua, black, and gray

New York Mets
Founded: 1962
Park: Shea Stadium
Park Opened: 1964
Colors: Black, blue, and orange

Philadelphia Phillies
Founded: 1883
Park: Citizens Bank Park
Park Opened: 2004
Colors: Red and white

Washington Nationals
Founded: 1969
Park: RFK Stadium
Park Opened: 1961
Colors: Red, white, and blue

The Braves have been the most successful team since the current version of the NL East was formed in 1994. But the division's other teams are closing the gap.

Montreal, the first major-league team outside of the United States, was an **expansion franchise** that year. The Expos were placed in the newly formed NL East along with the Chicago Cubs, the New York Mets, the Philadelphia Phillies, the Pittsburgh Pirates, and the St. Louis Cardinals. A seventh team, the expansion Florida Marlins, was added to the NL East in 1993. The following year, the league reorganized into three divisions—East, West, and Central.

In the new alignment, the Braves shifted from the West to the more geographically appropriate East. The Cubs, Pirates, and Cardinals moved over to the Central Division. And the Marlins, Expos, Mets, and Phillies stayed in the East to join the Braves in a five-team division. The lone change since then came following the 2004 season, when the Expos moved from Montreal to Washington, D.C., and became known as the Nationals.

Read on to learn more about all of the teams in today's NL East.

The Phillies and the Marlins made strong surges in the second half of the 2006 season, but both teams fell short of reaching the postseason.

THE ATLANTA BRAVES

Since the Braves won the NL West Division championship in Bobby Cox's first full season as manager in 1991, no other team in major-league baseball has had as much sustained success. Indeed, the Braves can stake a claim as MLB's unofficial "Team of the '90s"—and the decade of the 2000s hasn't been so bad either. Then again, the Braves' franchise has found success throughout its long history, whether it be in Boston, Milwaukee, or Atlanta.

The Braves celebrated after winning the 1995 World Series. Their six-game victory over the Indians marked their first championship since moving to Atlanta in 1966.

CHAPTER ONE

That history began way back in 1871 in Boston. Players such as Hall of Famer Hugh Duffy, whose .440 batting average in 1894 is a single-season record that likely will never be broken, helped the club win eight pennants in the pre-World Series era (before 1903). The franchise played under a variety of nicknames while in Boston, including Red Caps, Beaneaters, Doves, and Rustlers, before becoming the Braves in 1912. They were known as the Bees for a brief period beginning in 1936 before **reverting** to Braves for good in 1941.

After sweeping the Philadelphia Athletics in four games to win its first World Series in 1914, Boston fell on hard times. It would be 34 years before the club won another NL pennant. It came in 1948, when Johnny Sain won 24 games and Warren Spahn won 15 for a Braves' squad that went 91–62 during the regular season, then lost to the Cleveland Indians in the World Series.

By 1952, the Braves had fallen to seventh place, and attendance in Boston had dropped greatly. Owner Lou Perini moved the club to Milwaukee after the 1952 season, marking the first change in the NL's eight-team setup since

The Braves won the first game in the history of the National League. It came on April 22, 1876. The visiting Braves, then based in Boston, scored twice in the top of the ninth inning to beat the Philadelphia Athletics, 6–5.

Warren Spahn won more career games (363) than any other lefthander in big-league history. When he and Johnny Sain combined to help the Braves win the National League pennant with little help from the club's other starters in 1948, a poem in the *Boston Post* coined the phrase, "Spahn and Sain and pray for rain."

This statue of Warren Spahn stands outside Turner Field in Atlanta. Spahn won more games—363 in his 21 seasons—than any other left-hander in history.

1900. As the franchise bounced back at the turnstiles, the club bounced back on the field, too. The Braves won 92 games their first season in Milwaukee in 1953—a whopping 28 more than they did in their final year in Boston in 1952. The Braves boasted the league's best pitching staff, led by Spahn, second-year pitcher Lew Burdette, and rookie Bob Buhl. Third baseman Eddie Mathews led the league in home runs.

In 1954, Hank Aaron, a star in the fading **Negro Leagues**, joined the Braves. In his 23-year big-league career (his first 21 seasons were with the Braves), he became the game's all-time leader with 755 home runs. In 1957, the Braves won the NL pennant by eight games, then beat the powerful Yankees in seven games in the World Series for their first championship since 1914.

"Hammerin' Hank" Aaron belted 755 home runs in his 23 big-league seasons. All but his final 22 (which came with the Brewers) were hit in a Braves' uniform.

Seldom-used Francisco Cabrera had only 10 big-league at-bats during the 1992 season, but he was called on to pinch hit in the bottom of the ninth inning of Game Seven of the National League Championship Series against Pittsburgh that year. Cabrera's bases-loaded single to left field scored David Justice with the tying run and Sid Bream with the winning run to give the Braves a 3–2 victory and their second consecutive pennant.

In his first full season as a closer, John Smoltz saved a National League-record 55 games in 2002. He became the Braves' career saves leader in 2004 (with 154) before returning to the starting rotation the next year.

The Braves won the pennant again the next year, but lost to the Yankees in the World Series. As the Braves fell from the top of the NL standings, attendance started to plummet. By 1965, attendance reached an all-time low. So the Braves moved again, this time to Atlanta, where they remain today.

The Braves' history in Atlanta began with three mediocre seasons. But with Aaron belting 44 home runs and Phil Niekro winning 23 games, the Braves won the NL West in the first season of that division's existence in 1969. The Braves' next success came in 1982, when they won the West—led by Niekro and slugger Dale Murphy. By 1990, however, the Braves had sunk to last place in the division.

The following year, Atlanta staged a "worst-to-first" comeback. The Braves captured the NL West, then won their first pennant in Atlanta, beating the Pirates in the NLCS. The 1991 Braves were led by a trio of young pitchers—Tom Glavine, Steve Avery, and John Smoltz—who would dominate the NL for years to come. Terry Pendleton, David Justice, and Ron Gant pro-

vided the offense. In the '91 World Series against the Minnesota Twins, the Braves lost a closely fought seven-game series.

The Braves took the NL West again in 1992 and 1993, but fell short of winning the World Series each time. In 1994, the Braves moved to the NL East. The following season, Atlanta won the division, and later beat Colorado and Cincinnati for the pennant. Then the Braves edged Cleveland to win their only World Series of the 1990s.

The Braves continued to win division title after division title even as different players came and went. Pitcher Greg Maddux, the reigning NL Cy Young winner, joined the Braves' strong staff in 1993, and

Right-hander John Smoltz has been a mainstay on the Braves' pitching staff since first joining the club as a 21-year-old rookie in 1988.

was the league's top pitcher three more years in a row. Sweet-swinging rookie Chipper Jones joined the team in 1995. In 1996, Smoltz captured the Cy Young Award. Center fielder Andruw Jones became a regular at age 20 in 1997. He averaged 34 home runs over the next 10 seasons, including a career-best 51 in 2005.

In recent years, a new cast of young players, such as first baseman Adam LaRoche and outfielder Jeff Francoeur, has emerged. Through it all, though, Cox guided the Braves to division titles each season until the New York Mets finally snapped the string in 2006.

The Braves may have missed the playoffs in 2006, but they still have lots to be optimistic about—such as young stars Adam LaRoche (facing camera) and Jeff Francoeur.

CHAPTER TWO

THE FLORIDA MARLINS

The Marlins' history is relatively brief compared to the other teams in the NL East, but their story is already filled with more ups and downs than a rollercoaster ride at a Florida amusement park. They have been to dizzying heights and suffered terrifying drops—with few pauses along the way.

Edgar Renteria got a lift from his teammates after driving in the winning run in the bottom of the 11th inning of Game Seven of the 1997 World Series.

The Marlins were an expansion franchise in 1993, when the NL added Florida and Colorado to its stable of 12 teams. Though the Marlins won just a modest 64 games their first year, they were on the fast track to the top of the baseball world. They won the World Series in just their fifth season of existence in 1997. At the time, it was the fastest rise to a championship in baseball history (the expansion Arizona Diamondbacks eventually won the World Series in just their fourth season in 2001).

Gary Sheffield was one of the Marlins' first stars. He arrived in Florida in 1993 in a trade that sent pitcher Trevor Hoffman to San Diego—a deal that worked out for both sides.

Florida capped its championship run with a thrilling seven-game victory over the AL's Cleveland Indians in the World Series in 1997. But the groundwork for that title was laid the previous winter. Already featuring stars such as outfielder Gary Sheffield, young shortstop Edgar Renteria, starting pitcher Kevin Brown, and **closer** Robb Nen, the four-year-old club signed veteran Jim Leyland to manage the team. Then came a barrage of free-agent signings in rapid succession: Moises Alou, Bobby Bonilla, John Cangelosi, Dennis Cook, Jim Eisenreich, and Alex Fernandez. Overnight, it seemed, the Marlins had one of the best teams in the league.

The Marlins fought the Atlanta Braves for the NL East title all through the 1997 season. Although the Braves took the division, the Marlins qualified for the postseason as the NL **wild-card team**. In the Division Series, the Marlins swept the Giants, then stunned the Braves, beating them in the NLCS in six games.

Rookie pitcher Livan Hernandez, who had **defected** from Cuba, was named the most valuable player (MVP) of the NLCS. He went on to repeat that honor in the World Series, which the

The Marlins were an expansion team in 1993, but baseball hardly was new to Miami. The city, in fact, got its first minor-league team in 1912, when the Miami Magicians joined the Class D East Florida State League. And, of course, many Major League teams long have trained in the area during the spring.

The Marlins won only 64 games their inaugural year in 1993, but All-Star closer Bryan Harvey saved 45 of them. No other reliever before or since shut the door in such a large percentage of his team's victories.

Kevin Brown was the Marlins' ace in 1996 and 1997. He won 16 games and struck out 205 batters for the club's '97 World Series champions.

Marlins won on Renteria's winning hit in the bottom of the 11th inning of Game Seven.

As quickly as the Marlins' fortunes' rose, however, they fell pre-
cipitously. Following the incredible 1997 season, team owner Wayne
Huizenga claimed that he had lost huge amounts of money on the team.
He immediately began getting rid of his best players. Then he sold the
team to businessman John Henry. After winning 92 games in 1997,

When pitcher Josh Beckett tagged out the Yankees' Jorge Posada for the final out in the 2003
World Series (above), the Marlins were champions for the second time.

When Marlins rookie Anibal Sanchez blanked Arizona 4–0 on September 6, 2006 without surrendering a hit, he ended the longest no-hitter drought in Major League history. It was the first big-league no-hitter since the Diamondbacks' Randy Johnson pitched a perfect game in 2004—a stretch of 6,364 games. Sanchez's gem was the fourth no-hitter, though, in the relatively brief history of the Marlins. In 1996, Al Leiter no-hit the Colorado Rockies 11–0, and the next year Kevin Brown was nearly perfect in a 9–0 rout of San Francisco (the Giants' lone baserunner came in the eighth inning, when outfielder Marvin Benard was hit by a pitch). In 2001, A.J. Burnett shut down the Padres without a hit in the Marlins' 3–0 victory.

the Marlins managed a meager 54 wins in 1998. Another last-place finish followed in 1999, too. Some players showed promise, however. In 2000, pitcher Ryan Dempster won 14 games and was selected to the All-Star team. Antonio Alfonseca led the majors with 45 saves. Luis Castillo led the majors with 62 stolen bases and batted .334 leading off. Outfielder Cliff Floyd and infielder Mike Lowell also helped the Marlins climb out of the **cellar**, finishing third.

Two fourth-place finishes preceded another magical season in 2003. After the club got off to a slow start, 72-year-old Jack McKeon replaced Jeff Torborg as the club's manager. Rookie left-hander Dontrelle Willis came up from the minors and confused NL hitters with his unusual pitching motion. The Marlins had the best record in the league over the last four months of the regular season to earn a wild-card berth. Then, after beating the Giants and the Cubs in the playoffs, Florida upset the New York Yankees in six games to win the World Series. Josh Beckett, a 23-year-old pitcher with unlimited potential, shut down the Yankees on five hits in the final game to secure the Marlins' second title in their brief history.

Most of the World Series stars soon were gone in another **dismantling** of the club, however, and the Marlins have struggled since to win as many games as they have lost. Throughout all the peaks and valleys, though, the Marlins have become known for a seemingly endless stockpile of young talent. The current headliners are third baseman Miguel Cabrera, second baseman Dan Uggla, and shortstop Hanley Ramirez. On the mound, youngsters such as Josh Johnson and Scott Olsen have joined Willis, the lone holdover among the starters from the 2003 championship team.

Acrobatic shortstop Hanley Ramirez is an up-and-coming star. He stole 51 bases for the Marlins in his first full big-league season in 2006.

THE NEW YORK METS

For much of their 45-season existence, the Mets have toiled in the lengthy shadow of the mighty Yankees, the American League (AL) team with whom they compete for the affections of New York baseball fans. From time to time, though, the Mets have emerged from those shadows to dominate the headlines in Big Apple newspapers. That includes in the 2006 season, when manager Willie Randolph's club ended the Braves' long reign atop the NL East by winning 97 regular-season games.

Manager Willie Randolph (center) and the Mets had lots to celebrate in 2006. They won the NL East and advanced all the way to Game Seven of the League Championship Series.

CHAPTER THREE

New York's recent success is a far cry from the original Mets, who were revered as lovable losers for their record-setting futility under Casey Stengel. In the club's expansion season of 1962, the Mets lost more games (120, against only 40 wins) than any other team did in one year in big-league history. Six more losing seasons followed.

Amazingly, New York fans—thrilled to have an NL club back in town after the Dodgers and Giants left for the West Coast following the 1957 season—took to this group of bumbling ball players. Over their first three years, the last-place Mets drew more fans in New York than the pennant-winning Yankees. In 1964, the Mets moved from the Polo Grounds (the former home of the New York Giants) into brand-new Shea Stadium. Despite continued dismal play, signs of hope were emerging by 1967. Mostly they were in the form of rookie pitcher Tom Seaver, who won 16 games, and new manager Gil Hodges. The next year, the Mets added lefty pitcher Jerry Koosman, who won 19 games.

Then, in 1969, the "Miracle Mets" shocked the baseball world by winning 100 regular-season games—a 27-game improvement over the previous

When the Mets came into being in 1962, they combined the uniform colors of the Dodgers (blue) and the Giants (orange and black). Those were the two teams that left New York following the 1967 season.

Gil Hodges already was a beloved figure in New York before managing the Mets to their first world championship in 1969. As a first baseman for the Brooklyn Dodgers in the 1940s and 1950s, he slugged more home runs (298) than any other right-hander in club history before leaving with the franchise when it moved to Los Angeles in 1958. Several years later, though, he returned to play for the expansion Mets in 1962.

The New York media called pitcher Tom Seaver "Tom Terrific." It's no wonder: He won 189 games in 11 seasons for the Mets.

23

year. After a slow start, New York was winning consistently by early summer. Future Hall of Famer Seaver had his best year, going 25–7 and winning the first of his three Cy Young Awards. The Mets won the NL East before sweeping the Atlanta Braves in the first National League Championship Series (NLCS). The Mets then pulled off a stunning upset of the Baltimore Orioles in the World Series. In only eight seasons, the Mets had gone from lovable losers to world champs.

Just before the start of the 1972 season, Hodges suffered a fatal heart attack. He was replaced by Yankees legend and Mets coach Yogi Berra. In 1973, the Mets won the NL East for the second time in the closest race of the 20th century. They beat Cincinnati to win their second pennant, but lost to Oakland in the World Series.

The next 10 years were terrible for the team. In 1980, Frank

Gary Carter was the backbone of the Mets' 1986 World Series champions. The fiery catcher eventually was inducted into the Hall of Fame (Class of 2003).

Robin Ventura hit a "grand-slam single" to win Game Five of the 1999 National League Championship Series against Atlanta. Down three games to one and facing elimination, the Mets fell behind 3–2 in the top of the 15th inning. But they pushed across one run, then sent Ventura to the plate with one out. His long fly ball cleared the fence in right field for an apparent walk-off grand slam. But jubilant teammates mobbed the Mets' third baseman before he could reach second base. The hit officially was ruled a single and one RBI, and New York won, 4–3. Unfortunately, the dramatic win only delayed the Mets' fate. Two night later, despite another New York rally, the Braves won Game Six 10–9 to clinch the series.

Cashen, who had built the Orioles into a powerhouse in the late 1960s, was brought in as general manager. Over the next few years, a combination of players from the farm system and some shrewd trades brought the Mets back into contention. In 1983, rookie slugger Darryl Strawberry arrived, and veteran first baseman Keith Hernandez came over from the Cardinals. The following year brought a new manager (former Oriole Davey Johnson), two rookie pitchers (Ron Darling and Dwight Gooden), and a second-place finish.

In 1985, catcher Gary Carter came over from the Expos. Gooden, at age 20, won the Cy Young Award with an astounding 24–4 record and an ERA of 1.53. The team again finished second, this time winning 98 games. In 1986, it all came together for the Mets. The team cruised to first place in the NL East with 108 victories. The postseason proved more difficult. The Mets won the NL pennant in a hard-fought series against Houston, including an epic 16-inning Game Six at the Astrodome. Then, one strike away from losing to the Red Sox in Game Six of the World Series, the Mets rallied. They won the game, then the Series, for their second championship.

The Mets returned to the postseason in 1988 with the same **core** from the '86 championship team, plus pitcher David Cone. Cone's 20–3 record and 2.22 ERA led the staff, but the Mets lost to the Dodgers in the NLCS. The early 1990s were a down period for the team. In 1996, Bobby Valentine took over as manager. In 1998, the Mets acquired pitcher Al Leiter and catcher Mike Piazza. Leiter would win 17 games for the Mets in '98, and Piazza remained baseball's premier offensive force among catchers. In 1999, the Mets returned to the postseason via the wild card. After beating Arizona in the Division Series, they lost to Atlanta in the NLCS. The following year, the Mets again won the wild card. This time, they beat the Giants in the Division Series and the Cardinals in the NLCS to win their first pennant since 1986.

David Cone was masterful during the 1988 season, when he won 20 games and lost only 3. He won 55 more games for the Mets over the next four years before he was traded.

The Mets' opponents in the 2000 World Series were the New York Yankees, setting up a "Subway Series" reminiscent of the classic Yankees-Dodgers and Yankees-Giants World Series of the 1950s. The Yankees beat their crosstown rivals in five games.

Following their appearance in the 2000 World Series, the Mets suffered through several disappointing years. By 2005, though, the club appeared primed for another championship run. Young stars were emerging such as electrifying shortstop and leadoff hitter Jose Reyes and third baseman David Wright, while the pitching staff was anchored by former Cy Young Award winners such as Pedro Martinez and Tom Glavine. The Mets won 83 games in Randolph's rookie year at the helm, then broke through to win the NL East in 2006 for the first time in 18 years.

Speedy shortstop Jose Reyes is one of baseball's most exciting players. He was a big reason the Mets won a National League-best 97 games during the 2006 season.

CHAPTER FOUR

THE PHILADELPHIA PHILLIES

Phillies relief pitcher Tug McGraw was nursing a 4–1 lead against the Royals in Game Six of the 1980 World Series when Kansas City's Willie Wilson stepped to the plate. The pressure of 97 years of history weighed on McGraw's left arm—97 years in which Philadelphia had failed to win a single world championship. McGraw struck out Wilson, ending the game and giving the Phillies a four games to two victory in the Series. The pitcher flung both arms in the air, and leapt for joy. It is the single-most **compelling** image in Phillies' annals.

Oh what a relief! Closer Tug McGraw jumped for joy after striking out Willie Wilson to end the 1980 World Series and give the Phillies their first championship ever.

The picture remains lasting not only because it gave Philadelphia the first Series title in its long history, but also because the Phillies haven't won another since. Though the franchise has played in the National League for more than 120 years, it remains Philadelphia's lone championship.

Still, that's not to say that the Phillies' history is not loaded with star players, colorful personalities, and winning teams—including a nine-season stretch from 1975 to 1983 in which Philadelphia consistently fielded some of baseball's best teams.

The Phillies' franchise began in 1883 when the team was known as the Quakers (they were not called the Phillies until 1890). That team managed to win only 17 of 98 games, but the Philadelphia teams of the late 1890s soon featured an outfield of Ed Delahanty, Billy Hamilton, and Sam Thompson, all of whom were future Hall of Famers. Another Hall of Famer, pitcher Grover Cleveland Alexander, arrived in 1911. He won 28 games that year and would go on to win 373 games in his 20-year career.

In 1915, Alexander posted a league-leading and career-best ERA of 1.22, helping the Phillies to their first pennant. After winning the opening game

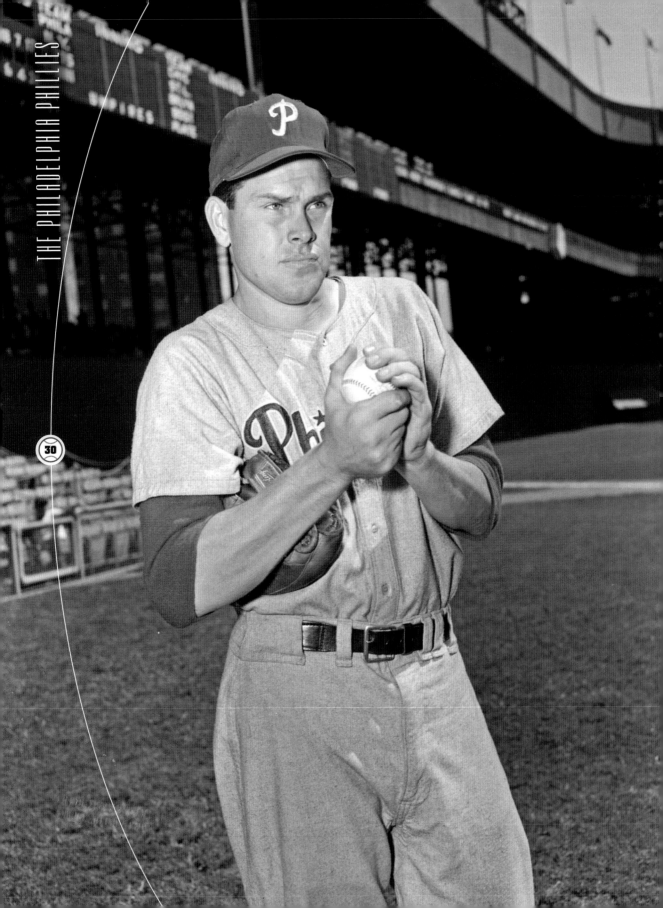

of the World Series, the Phillies dropped four in a row to the Boston Red Sox to lose the series.

After Alexander won 30 games in 1917 (the team finished second), the club traded him to Chicago. The next 30 or so years were dark ones for the Phillies. In the late 1940s, though, the Phillies became known for their "Whiz Kids"—first baseman Dick Sisler, outfielder Richie Ashburn, and pitchers Curt Simmons and Robin Roberts. Led by the Whiz Kids, the Phillies won their second pennant in 1950 but were frustrated in the World Series, getting swept by the Yankees in four straight games.

Roberts starred for the team for the next decade. He led the league in wins four consecutive seasons, beginning with a career-best 28 victories in 1952, but the Phillies rarely were a serious threat to win the pennant. By the end of the 1950s, they had plunged to the NL cellar. In 1961, they lost 23 straight games, the longest losing streak in the 20th century.

In 1964, pitcher Jim Bunning and slugger Richie Allen helped the Phillies build a big first-place lead in August. But 10 straight late-September losses helped blow the pennant. The 1970s brought the arrival of arguably the greatest

Hall of Fame pitcher Robin Roberts was just 23 years old when he won 20 games for the Phillies' 1950 National League pennant winners.

pitcher and greatest hitter the Phillies have ever had. In 1972, they got lefty Steve Carlton from St. Louis. He won 27 games that year for the last-place team, capturing his first Cy Young Award. In 1974, second-year third baseman Mike Schmidt blossomed into one of the league's premier power hitters. Together, they would lead the Phillies into the finest years in the club's long history.

In 1976, the team had its best regular season ever, winning 101 games and the NL East. The Phillies won the division again the following year. In 1978, they won their third straight East title, but lost for the third straight time in the NLCS. Dallas Green took over as manager in 1979, and veteran Pete Rose joined the team that year.

In 1980, it all came together for the Phillies. Schmidt led the league by hitting 48 home runs and driving in 121 runs, and Carlton topped

Third baseman Mike Schmidt played his entire 18-year big-league career in Philadelphia. He blasted 548 home runs, including 30 or more in 13 seasons.

the NL with 24 wins and 286 strikeouts. Philadelphia won two of three games from division-rival Montreal on the final weekend to win the NL East by a single game. After beating Houston in the NLCS, the Phillies downed the Royals in the World Series.

In 1982, the Phillies finished second. Carlton, though, won another Cy Young Award, becoming the first pitcher ever to win the award four times. The following year, the Phillies won their fourth NL pennant, but lost the World Series to Baltimore. The Phillies' golden years were about to end. Schmidt retired with 548 home runs. Carlton, who eventually

Steve Carlton won 329 games in 24 big-league seasons. Most of his success came with the Phillies, for whom he played from 1972 to 1986.

played for several big-league teams near the end of his career, retired in 1988 with 4,136 strikeouts, second all-time only to Nolan Ryan.

The Phillies won their fifth pennant in 1993, beating Atlanta in the NLCS, but they lost to Toronto in the World Series. The 1990s saw the rise of pitching star Curt Schilling, and hitting stars Bobby Abreu and Jim Thome shined in the early 2000s.

The 2006 season was another disappointing one for a Phillies' team that expected to contend for the division title but fell short of expectations. Still, the season was notable for the emergence of the club's latest star in slugger Ryan Howard. After Thome was traded before the season to make room for the young first baseman, Howard stepped in to hit 58 home runs in his first full year as a starter.

Ryan Howard tips his helmet to the home fans. They were showing their appreciation for one of his club-record 58 home runs in 2006.

CHAPTER FIVE

35

THE WASHINGTON NATIONALS

It is ironic that the club that has played more international games than any other team in major-league history relocated to America's capital in time for the 2005 season. But after years of searching, the franchise hopes it has found a permanent home. Washington fans, starved for major-league baseball since the AL's Washington Senators left to become the Texas Rangers following the 1971 season, hope so, too.

Baseball returned to the nation's capital in the 2005 season when the Nationals hosted the Arizona Diamondbacks in their home opener at RFK Stadium.

The Nationals began their baseball lives as the expansion Montreal Expos in 1969. (In case you're wondering, the Expos got their name from "Expo '67," the World's Fair that recently had been held in Montreal.) Fans north of the border responded with a show of national pride, turning out in excellent numbers despite less-than-excellent play on the field. Young outfielder Rusty Staub batted .302 for Montreal, but the team managed to win only 52 games. Still, the club drew 1.2 million fans and had plenty of hope for the future.

The Expos finished no better than fifth place in each of their first four seasons, but by 1973 they were in the midst of an incredibly tight race in the NL East. Ken Singleton drove in 103 runs that year. Rookie pitcher Steve Rogers put together a 1.54 ERA. Reliever Mike Marshall set a major-league record with 92 appearances, saving a league-leading 31 games. Though the Expos wound up in fourth place, they finished only 3 1/2 games behind the division-champion Mets.

The optimism from that season quickly **dissipated**, however, as Montreal sunk back to last place in 1975 and 1976. The next year, the team moved from Jarry Park into brand-new Olympic

The first home run in franchise history was hit by a pitcher—and it came against future Hall of Famer Tom Seaver, no less! Reliever Dan McGinn hit the historic blast in the expansion Expos' inaugural game in 1969. Montreal beat the Mets 11–10 at Shea Stadium in New York.

The Expos' first home venue was Jarry Park. It was a 3,000-seat city park that was expanded to accommodate 28,500 fans in time for the home opener in 1969. In 1977, the club moved into Olympic Stadium.

The Expos had little trouble producing All-Stars, as this photo from the 1982 All-Star Game shows. Montreal only had trouble holding on to them.

Stadium, which had been built for the 1976 Summer Olympics. The same year, Dick Williams took over as manager. Williams had guided the Oakland A's to back-to-back World Series victories in 1972 and 1973. The Expos also added veteran slugger Tony Perez, rookie outfielder Andre Dawson, and catcher Gary Carter. Perez and Carter eventually were inducted into baseball's Hall of Fame.

In 1980, the Expos were tied for first place heading into the final series of the year. The Phillies took two of three from Montreal in that series to win the division title by a single game. In the split season (due to a players' strike) of 1981, Montreal won the NL East in the second half of the year. The Expos captured their first NL East crown by beating Philadelphia in a special playoff. But they lost to the Dodgers in the NLCS.

Andre Dawson was the NL rookie of the year while with Montreal in 1977. Eventually, he became a league MVP—unfortunately, it was with the Chicago Cubs.

In 1988 and '89, the Expos got off to fast starts, spending time in first place in the NL East, before slumping to .500 finishes (81–81) in each season. Under new manager Felipe Alou, the Expos climbed from fifth place to second in 1992. They were led by pitchers Ken Hill and Dennis Martinez, and outfielder Larry Walker, who went on to become one of the game's best hitters. In 1993, the team again finished second, compiling an impressive 94–68 record.

On August 7, 1994, the Expos were not only in first place in the NL East, but they also had the best record in Major League Baseball. A postseason appearance seemed certain. Then, less than a week later, the players went on strike, and the rest of the season—and the postseason—was canceled. In 1995, the Expos dropped into last place. The gulf between the wealthy big-market teams and the smaller-market clubs, which could not compete for expensive free agents, was beginning to hurt the Expos. In 1997, Pedro Martinez became the first Expos pitcher to win the Cy Young Award. But the team could not afford to keep Martinez, as well as some of their top offensive players.

In 1998, two young stars emerged. Power-hit-

ting outfielder Vladimir Guerrero and closer Ugueth Urbina led the club to a fourth-place finish. New ownership in 1999 didn't help the Expos' financial difficulties. Things got worse in 2000, despite the fact that Guerrero broke his own team records with a .345 batting average and 44 homers.

In 2002, the club was on the verge of being dissolved before Major League Baseball took over ownership of the Expos. Hall of Fame slugger and veteran manager Frank Robinson was named the team's **skipper**. In 2003, the Expos played 22 "home" games at Hiram Bithorn Stadium in San Juan, Puerto Rico. Finally, the club's uncertain future was resolved with the move to Washington, D.C.

Though the club was not expected to be much of a factor in the NL East race their first year as the Nationals, Robinson kept a team largely devoid of stars in the race until late in the season. Outfielder Jose Guillen

All-Star outfielder Vladimir Guerrero was a gifted player who could do it all—whether at the plate, on the basepaths, or in the field.

led the offense by hitting 27 home runs, while Livan Hernandez, the former World Series star of the Marlins, won 15 games on the mound. The next year, leadoff hitter Alfonso Soriano added both punch and speed to the top of the lineup, but the Nationals got off to a poor start and were never in the division chase.

Still, the fans in Washington welcomed back Major League Baseball with open arms. More than 2.7 million people watched the club in 2005 at RFK Stadium, the old home of football's Washington Redskins. The Nationals were scheduled to move into their new baseball-only ballpark in time for the 2008 season.

The Nationals hope that youngsters such as Ryan Zimmerman, who belted 20 home runs and drove in 110 runs at age 21 in 2006, will help turn around the franchise's fortunes.

STAT STUFF

TEAM RECORDS (THROUGH 2006)

Team	All-time Record	World Series Titles (Most Recent)	Number of Times in the Postseason	Top Manager (Wins)
Atlanta*	9,837–9,699	3 (1995)	21	Bobby Cox (1,816)
Florida	1,041–1,160	2 (2003)	2	Jack McKeon (241)
N.Y. Mets	3,408–3,742	2 (1986)	7	Davey Johnson (595)
Philadelphia	8,764–9,956	1 (1980)	9	Gene Mauch (646)
Washington**	2,907–3,115	0	1	Felipe Alou (691)

*includes Boston and Milwaukee
**includes Montreal

NATIONAL LEAGUE EAST CAREER LEADERS (THROUGH 2006)

ATLANTA

Category	Name (Years with Team)	Total
Batting Average	Hugh Duffy (1891–1900)	.332
Home Runs	Hank Aaron (1954–1974)	733
RBI	Hank Aaron (1954–1974)	2,202
Stolen Bases	Herman Long (1890–1902)	433
Wins	Warren Spahn (1942, 1946–1964)	356
Saves	John Smoltz (1988–2006)	154
Strikeouts	Phil Niekro (1964–1983, 1987)	2,912

NATIONAL LEAGUE EAST CAREER LEADERS (THROUGH 2006)

FLORIDA

Category	Name (Years with Team)	Total
Batting Average	Miguel Cabrera (2003–06)	.311
Home Runs	Mike Lowell (1999–2005)	143
RBI	Mike Lowell (1999–2005)	578
Stolen Bases	Luis Castillo (1996–2005)	281
Wins	Dontrelle Willis (2003–06)	58
Saves	Robb Nen (1993–97)	108
Strikeouts	A.J. Burnett (1999–2005)	753

43

NEW YORK

Category	Name (Years with Team)	Total
Batting Average	John Olerud (1997–99)	.315
Home Runs	Darryl Strawberry (1983–1990)	252
RBI	Darryl Strawberry (1983–1990)	733
Stolen Bases	Mookie Wilson (1980–89)	281
Wins	Tom Seaver (1967–1977, 1983)	198
Saves	John Franco (1990–2004)	276
Strikeouts	Tom Seaver (1967–1977, 1983)	2,541

MORE STAT STUFF

NATIONAL LEAGUE EAST CAREER LEADERS (THROUGH 2006)

PHILADELPHIA

Category	Name (Years with Team)	Total
Batting Average	Billy Hamilton (1890–95)	.361
Home Runs	Mike Schmidt (1972–1989)	548
RBI	Mike Schmidt (1972–1989)	1,595
Stolen Bases	Billy Hamilton (1890–95)	508
Wins	Steve Carlton (1972–1986)	241
Saves	Jose Mesa (2001–03)	111
Strikeouts	Steve Carlton (1972–1986)	3,031

WASHINGTON

Category	Name (Years with Team)	Total
Batting Average	Vladimir Guerrero (1996–2003)	.323
Home Runs	Vladimir Guerrero (1996–2003)	234
RBI	Tim Wallach (1980–1992)	905
Stolen Bases	Tim Raines (1979–1990, 2001)	635
Wins	Steve Rogers (1973–1985)	158
Saves	Jeff Reardon (1981–86)	152
Strikeouts	Steve Rogers (1973–1985)	1,621

GLOSSARY

ace–the best starting pitcher on a team

cellar–last place

closer–a relief pitcher brought in at the end of a game to save a victory for his team

compelling–interesting or captivating

core–central, or basic, part

defected–left a country because of disapproval of its political policies

dismantling–taking apart, disassembling

dissipated–went away or was squandered

expansion franchise–a new team that starts from scratch, thus increasing (or expanding) the total number of clubs in a given league

Negro Leagues–baseball leagues that existed from the 1920s through the 1950s; teams were composed of African American players, who were barred until 1947 from playing in the major leagues

resurgence–rising up, or being successful again

reverting–going back to

skipper–an informal term for a manager

wild-card team–a team that finishes in second place in its division but still makes the playoffs by virtue of having the best record among a league's non-division winners

TIMELINE

1876 The Braves franchise becomes a charter member of the newly formed National League.

1883 The Phillies franchise debuts in Philadelphia; the club is known as "the Quakers."

1953 The Braves move from Boston to Milwaukee.

1962 The New York Mets debut but lose a record 120 games.

1966 The Braves move from Milwaukee to Atlanta.

1969 Baseball expands to Canada for the first time when Montreal debuts as an expansion team.

The "Miracle Mets" win their first World Series in only their eighth season.

1980 In their 98th season, the Phillies win the World Series for the first time.

1986 One strike away from elimination, the Mets rally to beat the Red Sox in Game 6 of the World Series, then take Game 7 to win their second championship.

1993 The Florida Marlins join the NL as an expansion team.

1995 The Braves win their third World Series, their first in Atlanta.

1997 In only their fifth season, the Marlins earn a wild-card playoff berth and go on to win the World Series.

2003 The surprising Marlins win the World Series for the second time in their brief history.

2005 The Expos franchise moves from Montreal to Washington, D.C.

FOR MORE INFORMATION

BOOKS

Dewey, Donald, and Nicholas Acocella. *The Encyclopedia of Major League Teams*. New York: HarperCollins, 1993.

Golenbock, Peter. *Amazin': The Miraculous History of New York's Most Beloved Baseball Team*. New York: Saint Martin's Press, 2002.

Jordan, David M. *Occasional Glory: The History of the Philadelphia Phillies*. Jefferson, N.C.: McFarland & Company, 2002.

Nichols, John. *The History of the Florida Marlins*. Mankato, Minn.: Creative Education, 1999.

Stewart, Wayne. *The History of the Atlanta Braves*. Mankato, Minn.: Creative Education, 2003.

ON THE WEB

Visit our home page for lots of links about the National League East teams: ***http://www.childsworld.com/links***
Note to Parents, Teachers, and Librarians: We routinely check our Web links to make sure they're safe, active sites—so encourage your readers to check them out!

INDEX

Aaron, Hank, 10
Alexander, Grover C., 29-31
Alfonseca, Antonio, 19
Atlanta Braves, 4, 6, 7-13
Beckett, Josh, 18, 19
Berra, Yogi, 24
Brown, Kevin, 16, 19
Bunning, Jim, 29, 31
Burnett, A.J., 19
Cabrera, Francisco, 11
Carlton, Steve, 32-33, 34
Carter, Gary, 24, 25, 38
Cashen, Gary, 24-25
Castillo, Luis, 19
Cone, David, 26
Coveleski, Harry, 29
Cox, Bobby, 7
Dempster, Ryan, 19
Duffy, Hugh, 8
Florida Marlins, 4, 14-20
Francoeur, Jeff, 13
Grimsley, Ross, 39
Guerrero, Vladimir, 40
Guillen, Jose, 40-41
Harvey, Bryan, 16
Hernandez, Livan, 16, 41
Hodges, Gil, 22, 24
Howard, Ryan, 31, 34
Huizenga, Wayne, 18
Jones, Andruw, 13
Jones, Chipper, 13
Justice, David, 11
Koosman, Jerry, 22
LaRoche, Andrew, 13
Leiter, Al, 19, 26
Leyland, Jim, 16
Maddux, Greg, 12-13
Marshall, Mike, 36

Martinez, Pedro, 27, 39
McGinn, Dan, 36
McGraw, Tug, 28
McKeon, Jack, 19
Montreal Expos, 6, 36-40
Murphy, Dale, 11
New York Mets, 4, 21-27
Niekro, Phil, 11
Philadelphia Phillies, 4,
   28-34
Piazza, Mike, 26
Ramirez, Hanley, 20
Randolph, Willie, 21
Renteria, Edgar, 14, 16, 18
Roberts, Robin, 31
Robinson, Frank, 40
Rogers, Steve, 36
Sain, Johnny, 8
Sanchez, Anibal, 19
Schmidt, Mike, 32, 33
Seaver, Tom, 22, 24, 36
Sheffield, Gary, 15, 16
Singleton, Ken, 36
Smoltz, John, 11, 12, 13
Soriano, Alfonso, 39, 41
Spahn, Warren, 8, 10
Staub, Rusty, 36
Stengel, Casey, 22
Thome, Jim, 34
Urbina, Ugueth, 40
Valentine, Bobby, 26
Ventura, Robin, 25
Walker, Larry, 39
Washington Nationals, 4, 6, 35-41
Williams, Dick, 38
Willis, Dontrelle, 19, 20
Wilson, Willie, 28
Zimmerman, Ryan, 41

48

ABOUT THE AUTHOR

Michael Teitelbaum has been a writer and editor of children's books and magazines for more than 20 years. Michael (a lifelong fan of the New York Mets and the New York Knicks) and his wife, Sheleigh, split their time between New York City and their 160-year-old farmhouse in the Catskill Mountains of upstate New York.